Summary and Analysis of

THE LIFE-CHANGING MAGIC OF TIDYING UP

The Japanese Art of Decluttering and Organizing

Based on the Book by Marie Kondo

WORTH BOOKS
SMART SUMMARIES

This Worth Books book is based on the 2014 ebook edition of *The Life-Changing Magic of Tidying Up: The Japanese Art of Decluttering and Organizing* by Marie Kondo published by Ten Speed Press.

Summary and analysis copyright © 2017 by Open Road Integrated Media, Inc.

ISBN: 978-1-5040-4667-1

Worth Books
180 Maiden Lane
Suite 8A
New York, NY 10038
www.worthbooks.com

WORTH BOOKS
SMART SUMMARIES

Worth Books is a division of Open Road Integrated Media, Inc.

Contents

Context

The Life-Changing Magic of Tidying Up author Marie Kondo had already written a college thesis titled "How to Declutter Your Apartment" and built up a successful consulting business when someone on her waiting list suggested she write a book. Her book proposal caught the eye of Tokyo-based publisher Tomohiro Takahashi, and was written and published in Japan in late 2010.

In March 2011, Japan was hit by the Tōhoku earthquake and tsunami. This natural disaster contributed to increased sales of the book, as many of those who were affected by the resulting damage were interested in taking stock of their lives and starting anew.

The book was translated and became a bestseller in both Germany and the United Kingdom before being published in the United States in October 2014. According to the *New York Times*, *The Life-Changing Magic of Tidying Up* was published "quietly and to zero fanfare and acclaim. Kondo's inability to speak English made promotional radio and talk-show appearances hard sells. But one day, a *New York Times* Home section reporter happened upon the book and wrote an article discussing her own attempt at konmariing her closets; the book caught fire."

Decluttering as a whole has become trendy in the United States, not just with Marie Kondo's book and philosophy but also with other popular efforts. A study done between 2001 and 2005 by researchers at UCLA found middle-class Americans facing a "clutter crisis." They attributed this crisis, in part, "to unprecedented access to deeply discounted consumer goods."

Receptivity to Marie Kondo may be attributed to a few factors: her easy-to-follow instructions and approachable writing style, word of mouth recommendations, and a cultural shift to mindfulness, self-reflection, and meditation. For some, the promise of being able to create an atmosphere of order and calm in a world that seems out of control and governed by chaos is a very tempting proposition.

Overview

KonMari is Marie Kondo's method for organizing your home, which encourages a shift in how you think about material possessions. This practice involves simplifying your surroundings so that they work for you and make you happy, and so that you can focus on what you want to do in life rather than being distracted by a cluttered, unfulfilling environment.

The process involves starting with where you are, addressing all of your stuff—piece-by-piece. Kondo stresses the importance of doing this category-by-category, rather than room-by-room, in a specific order. Keep items that "spark joy," and discard those that don't give you that feeling of happiness. Use simple storage solutions designed to make your possessions comfortable in their designated places, and to make your life easier. The best part? You'll only have to do it once—and Kondo claims you will never go back to a disorderly environment at home.

Tidying in this way is a process of gaining self-knowledge that can have a dramatic effect on your life. Kondo calls it "magic."

Summary

Introduction

Marie Kondo explains her background and introduces the KonMari tidying method as a concept. She shares some testimonials from former clients who are now "surrounded only by the things they love." Reorganizing your home can shift your entire lifestyle and perspective in ways that are "transforming."

Chapter One: Why can't I keep my house in order?

It's assumed that we all know how to organize possessions and physical spaces naturally. After all, shelter is one of the most basic human needs. But, as with learning how to cook, this is a skill one needs to be taught.

With the KonMari method, you will undertake a "tidying marathon" of your entire home that should be completed within six months. This mission should be treated as a special event, not a chore, because it's the first step in shifting your mindset and creating the lifestyle that you want. If you aim for perfection the first time, you won't rebound. Kondo claims that if you tidy a little each day, you'll be tidying forever. But if you go through the KonMari process, you will reset your lifestyle once and for all.

The KonMari method—essentially, discarding, then storing—works for everybody, regardless of your personality, because it empowers you to make your own decisions.

When tidying, a common mistake is to sort by room. In the KonMari method, you "sort by category, not by location." Because people often keep the same type of thing in more than one room or place in the house, tidying by location means you'll always be tidying.

Set goals for tidying one category at a time: clothes, papers, etc. Furthermore, it's important not to be distracted by fancy storage methods. There can be no proper storage method without first discarding the things that you don't need—otherwise you'll still have clutter, it will just be out of sight.

Once you've gone through this process and put everything in its place, the only thing you'll have to do on a daily basis is put things back where they belong.

Need to Know: Tidying is an important life skill that most of us don't have by nature—and many of the things that we have been taught about tidying are actually holding us back. The KonMari method of doing a big tidying overhaul, which includes first discarding, then storing properly, works for everyone and only needs to be done once.

Chapter Two: Finish discarding first

"Before you start, visualize your destination." Think about why you picked up this book, and visualize—in concrete terms—what it would be like to live in the space that you desire. Then, ask yourself why this is what you're looking for—because this will help you determine "the reasons behind your ideal lifestyle." For most, it's some variation of being happy, but each of us needs to realize this for ourselves.

The selection criterion during the discarding process is simple. "The best way to choose what to keep and what to throw away is to take each item in one's hand and ask: 'Does this spark joy?' If it does, keep it. If not, dispose of it." This is perhaps the most famous tenet of the KonMari tidying philosophy, and it is absolutely necessary to the process. Marie Kondo believes that your body reacts to the things you love, that you can feel it. You instinctively know the items that you want to be surrounded by.

Tidy in this order, one category at a time: clothes, books, papers, *komono* (miscellany), and mementos. Kondo designed this list from easiest to most difficult to discard, so that you can work your way up to the tougher decisions. Take care with each item, really considering if each sparks joy in you and has a purpose in your life. Don't worry about being wasteful. Let each item you discard go with gratitude. Discarding helps you appreciate the things that you do care about.

Tidying can be a form of meditation. Ideally, don't listen to music while you tidy so you can pay attention to your inner dialogue. Start in the early morning, with a clear mind. Don't involve your family—and don't show people what you're discarding, because they'll be tempted to burden themselves with things *they* don't need.

Need to Know: Tidy by category, and in this order: clothes, books, papers, *komono* (miscellany), and mementos. Discard before you begin to store. Choose which items to keep rather than which to get rid of by touching each possession and asking yourself if it sparks joy. If it doesn't, discard it. Complete your KonMari within six months.

Chapter Three: Tidying by category works like magic

"Place every item of clothing in the house on the floor," then sort in the following order: tops, bottoms, clothes that should be hung, socks, underwear, bags, accessories, clothes for specific events, shoes. Kondo claims, "Downgrading [items] to 'loungewear' is taboo." If you aren't willing to wear something out of the house, it's probably because it doesn't spark joy in you.

Clothing storage is important, and folding things correctly, using the KonMari method, will "solve your storage problems." Folding can allow you to fit anywhere from two to four times the number of clothing items in a space compared to hanging them. Plus, if you fold things properly, they will last longer. Store things standing up, rather than flat, because it allows you to see what you have all in one glance, and it's better for your clothing.

The process varies from item to item, but you should essentially try to get everything into "a simple, smooth rectangle" that can stand on its edge. If something will be stored in a drawer, fold it to fit the drawer. Thin, soft material should be folded more tightly than thick, fluffy material. Kondo feels strongly about the proper storage of socks, because they work hard for us all day. They are resting when they're in the drawer, but they can't rest well if you ball or tie them up—fold them as you do the rest of your clothing. Additionally, shoeboxes make great drawer dividers.

While most things should be folded, some clothes look happier hung, so hang them. Keep categories together (e.g., jackets with jackets), and arrange all of the hanging items so that they rise to the right. This means heavy, dark items should be on the left, and light, bright items should be on the right. "By category, coats would be on the far left, followed by dresses, jackets, pants, skirts, and blouses." Avoid storing off-season clothing separately from in-season clothing, if possible.

Kondo acknowledges that books are often very difficult for people to let go of. Put them on the floor and, just as with the review of your clothes, touch each one to determine which spark joy—don't start reading. If there are too many books to put on the floor at once, sort using these four categories: "general (books you read for pleasure); practical (references, cookbooks, etc.); visual (photograph collections, etc.); magazines."

You aren't going to read very many of your books again, and they don't serve much purpose sitting on a shelf. Get rid of any books that don't spark joy. Also, if you haven't read a book yet, chances are you won't and you don't need it. If you really want an unread or reference book after you've gotten rid of it, buy another copy and make a point to read it. Having fewer books around can make the books you do have more impactful.

The rule of thumb with papers is to discard almost everything—except what you absolutely have to keep. There is a specific prescribed order for sorting *komono* as well: "Keep things because you love them—not 'just because.'" Get rid of gifts that don't suit you, as the true meaning of gifts "is to be received." Respect loose change—because coins are useful money—by putting it in your wallet and using it. Don't use a piggybank.

Going through sentimental items allows you to process your past in order to be able to live fully in the present. You will remember your favorite moments even if you no longer have the mementos to go with them. If you send a box "home" to your parents, you'll never open it again . . . so you may as well discard it. While sorting photographs, remove them from albums so you can look at them individually. Keep only those that "touch your heart."

"Only you can know what kind of environment makes you feel happy." That's why Kondo's advice is more feeling-based than numerically prescriptive. Trust yourself.

Need to Know: Folding and hanging clothes properly is key to storing them successfully. In general, you should discard a large number of your books, including those you haven't read yet, as well as the vast majority of your papers. Most of your *komono* (incidental items) likely do not spark joy and should be discarded. Mementos are the most difficult to sort, but doing so allows you to process your past and, therefore, to live in the present. Trust yourself and you will reach a point at which your surroundings make you happy.

Chapter Four: Storing your things to make your life shine

"Designate a place for each thing." Do this once and stick with it. Store items in the same category near each other. Go for simple storage solutions, such as drawers and boxes. Round storage solutions waste space. Ask your house and your belongings where and how they ought to be stored. Designate spaces for both storage and sanctuary for each person in the house. Empty your bag every day and store your bags in each other—let the straps dangle so you can see which bags are there. Keep things off of the floor and out of the bath and the kitchen sink; tuck them into closets or cupboards instead.

Think of your possessions as parts of your life rather than just "things." When you buy new clothes, take them out of their packages and remove the tags right away. Not only do clothes take up less space when they are out of their packaging, they also feel less like products and more like possessions when their tags are removed.

Before buying in bulk, consider the cost of storage. Always thank your stuff; we enjoy having a home, and so do our belongings.

Need to Know: Give each item its own a place near other things of a similar type, using a simple storage solution. Shoeboxes are recommended. Tuck things away when not in use and be mindful of visual clutter. Empty your bag when you get home every day; store bags in one another. Remove tags and packaging when you purchase new items so they feel like possessions rather than products. Thank your possessions and your home.

Chapter Five: The magic of tidying dramatically transforms your life

By deciding what you want to own, you're deciding the type of life you want to have. The process of consciously choosing the objects that you surround yourself with helps you become closer to knowing your true self. Many people who have followed the Kon-Mari method have become more passionate about their professions, hobbies, and home lives.

The process of tidying can be difficult because we have to "confront our imperfections and inadequacies and the foolish choices we made in the past." But that's better than denial, by either "letting things pile up" or "dumping things indiscriminately."

Most people surround themselves with things they don't need. It's much less stressful to find things when you've pared down—and everything will be OK even if you don't have what you want.

Marie Kondo suggests that there is a relationship between how you keep your home and the well-being of your physical body. Detoxing your home can lead to a body detox. In fact, many people who follow the KonMari method lose weight. Often the part of the body affected corresponds to the area of the home that is put in order (e.g., clear mind when books and documents have been discarded).

Lastly, Kondo believes that "your real life begins after putting your house in order." Tidy quickly so that you can move on to your true purpose.

Need to Know: Tidying is a process of gaining self-knowledge, and the resulting shift in mindset can be dramatic. This is what Kondo means by "magic."

Direct Quotes & Analysis

"The work involved can be broadly divided into two kinds: deciding whether or not to dispose of something and deciding where to put it."

These are the two basic steps of the KonMari method—discarding and storing—and they have to be done in this order. While it sounds simple, it's tedious work because you must examine each and every single thing you own, and then give each of the things you decide to keep a home; however, once you've completed the process, you never have to do it again.

"When your room is clean and uncluttered, you have no choice but to examine your inner state."

Marie Kondo argues that we clutter spaces as a form of distraction, so that we can avoid dealing with our problems. On the flip side, decluttering your physical space also declutters the mind, allowing you to process your feelings and, eventually, focus on living the life you want to live. A peaceful environment enables a peaceful mind.

"One reason so many of us never succeed at tidying is because we have too much stuff. This excess is caused by our ignorance of how much we actually own."

In high school, Kondo realized that the "tidy by location" method didn't work when she found a drawer in one room that had similar contents to a drawer in another room. It's hard to keep track of exactly what you have when the same or similar items are stored all over the house. Further, if you have items that are no longer useful to you, there is no need to hold on to them just because you can. Having fewer possessions enables us to appreciate what we do have in a different and satisfying manner.

"In addition to the physical value of things, there are three other factors that add value to our belongings: function, information, and emotional attachment."

The order in which you review your possessions is very intentional. By starting with items that are easier to make decisions about—such as clothes, which are much easier to replace than, say, photographs—you can develop your decision-making skills to the point where it will be easier to deal with your mementos and keepsakes.

"Papers are organized into only three categories: needs attention, should be saved (contractual documents), and should be saved (others)."

The rule of thumb here is to discard all papers except those that you absolutely have to keep, out of some form of obligation or duty—those that fall into the categories above. She finds papers annoying and claims that they can never inspire joy, though holding on to special ones, such as your favorite love letters or personal journals with great sentimental value, may be saved.

"It is not our memories but the person we have become because of those past experiences that we should trea-sure. This is the lesson these keepsakes teach us when we sort them. The space in which we live should be for the person we are becoming now, not for the person we were in the past."

This is how Kondo justifies the discarding of memen-tos. She thinks that sorting through these special items and touching each one allows you to process your past, put it behind you, and then move forward into the future. Consider this sentiment an opportunity to reflect on who you are in the present.

"Clutter has only two possible causes: too much effort is required to put things away or it is unclear where things belong."

Proper storage—using Kondo's method—should solve these problems. Step one: you may ask yourself if you are simply being lazy. Step two: consider the old adage "A place for everything and everything in its place." Step three: act accordingly.

Trivia

1. Tidying has been part of her life since the age of five.

2. When she was fifteen, Kondo found and read *The Art of Discarding* by Nagisa Tatsumi, and it was a major catalyst for the development of her method. Unfortunately for English-speaking Konverts (those who ascribe to the KonMari method), this book doesn't seem to have been translated into English yet.

3. While she was in university, Kondo discovered Sari Solden's book *Women with Attention Deficit*

Disorder, which included commentary on women for whom the disorder affects their ability to tidy their homes. This contributed to her belief that keeping an orderly home is inherently psychological.

4. After KonMari, Kondo's clients are usually left with one-quarter to one-third of the clothes they started with.

5. Marie Kondo has a handful of American celebrity fans, including Jamie Lee Curtis, who wrote Kondo's profile for her *Time* Most Influential Person nomination, and Kate Hudson, who posted a photo of the book as well as a recommendation in the caption on her Instagram.

6. Marie Kondo keeps about thirty books in her collection at a time.

7. The record for most stuff discarded goes to one couple who worked with Marie Kondo to tidy their average-sized home, during which they got rid of two hundred bags of stuff as well as ten things that were too big for bags. Kondo estimates her clients have gotten rid of over 28,000 bags full of more than one million items.

8. You, too, can help to "organize the world." Kon-Mari Media now offers a training program for those who want to be certified in the KonMari method.

9. There is a subreddit dedicated to discussion of all things KonMari: https://www.reddit.com/r/kon-mari/

10. You can spark joy in your digital life: Consider the photos you keep on your smartphone or computer, and all of the emails that you've been collecting. Review them one by one and ask yourself if each should be kept or deleted.

What's That Word?

Dobutsu uranai: A method of fortune-telling based on zoology; each date of the calendar is associated with a particular animal, and each animal is associated with a specific personality type. Marie Kondo once considered this and other criteria for designing custom tidying methods for different personalities, but decided that only one system was needed.

Ikki ni: Japanese term that translates to "in one go"—or the way Marie Kondo recommends you tackle your home reorganization.

Komono: Small, miscellaneous items; accessories; odds and ends. Examples are: old batteries, buttons, makeup, stationery, and power cords.

KonMari: A contraction of Marie Kondo's name in the Japanese style (Kondo Mariko) and the name she's given to her tidying method. Variations of KonMari can be used as a noun or a verb (e.g., "konmariing" or "kondo'd").

Konverts: Those who ascribe to the KonMari method; KonMari devotees; super-fans.

Koromogae: A period of time when people switch to summer clothes in Japan, when winter clothes are packed away and summer clothes are brought out. It usually happens during Japan's rainy season in June. According to the book, *koromogae* "originated in China and was introduced to Japan as a court custom during the Heian period (794–1185 AD)." In the late 19th century, businesses and schools adopted the custom by switching to summer uniforms at this time. Marie Kondo doesn't believe there's a use for this tradition anymore. With air conditioning and heating, many of our clothing items are in use year-round, and with proper storage methods there's no reason to pack away off-season clothes.

Tatami: Thick, woven straw mats measuring about two meters in length and one meter in width, often found in traditional Japanese rooms. Rooms are commonly measured by how many *tatami* they could hold.

Te-ate: The Japanese word for healing, which literally means "to apply hands." Before modern medicine, people believed that healing could come through touching injuries, transferring energy from one person's hands onto the other's skin. Modern studies have shown physical touch to have a positive impact on the healing process (think: massage therapy). Kondo believes touching our clothing and objects is important because it gives our possessions some of our energy and makes them feel alive and cared for.

Tokimeku: "Spark joy" is the chosen translation for this Japanese word in the original text. It translates more directly to "flutter, palpitate, throb." This is the ultimate criteria for keeping or discarding any item you possess: Ask yourself if it sparks joy.

Critical Response

- A #1 *New York Times* bestseller
- An Amazon Best Book of 2014 in Crafts, Home & Garden

"[It is] enough to salute Kondo for her recognition of something quietly profound: that mess is often about unhappiness, and that the right kind of tidying can be a kind of psychotherapy for the home as well as for the people in it. . . . Its strength is its simplicity."

—*The Times* (London)

"All hail the new decluttering queen Marie Kondo, whose mess-busting best seller has prompted a craze for tidying in homes across the world. . . . One proper clear out is all you need for the rest of your life."   —*Good Housekeeping* (UK)

"A literal how-to-heave-ho, and I recommend it for anyone who struggles with the material excess of living in a privileged society. (Thanks to Ms. Kondo, I kiss my old socks goodbye.) To show you how serious my respect for Ms. Kondo is: if I ever get a tattoo, it will say, Spark Joy!"   —Jamie Lee Curtis,
Time

"How could this pocket-sized book, which has already sold over two million copies and sits firmly atop the *New York Times* Best Seller list, make such a big promise? Here's the short answer: Because it's legit . . . Kondo's method really can change your life—if you let it."
—Today.com

"This book is a cult. A totally reasonable, scary cult that works, doesn't kill people (a bonus), but does drastically change your life. In this case—for the better."
—BuzzFeed

"The method's anchoring principle, that we hang onto only what 'sparks joy,' deftly reconfigures the notion of tidying and decluttering as mere throwing away: transformative existential keeping seems to be Kondo's lesson."   —*The New Yorker*

"Kondo's thesis—that the world is filled with worthy recipients of mercy, including lightweight-microfiber ones—is as lovely as it is alien. It's empathy as an extreme sport."   —"The Cut," *New York Magazine*

"The cyclical purging of things you no longer use is not a new phenomenon. However, Kondo's way of anthropomorphizing belongings and paying them the respect of taking them out of the closet for a proper dismissal makes a big difference."   —*Vogue*

"Joy points upward, according to Marie Kondo, whose name is now a verb and whose nickname is being trademarked and whose life has become a philosophy."   —*The New York Times*

About Marie Kondo

Marie Kondo is a Japanese author and tidying consultant. She started tidying professionally at the age of nineteen, yet already has more than a decade of experience. Her husband, Takumi Kawahara, is her manager and photographer. Kondo has published five books in Japan and three in America, where she was named one of *Time*'s 100 Most Influential People of 2015 and one of *Fast Company*'s Most Creative People of 2015.

Kondo was the middle child of three and claims to have started tidying from age five, when *feng shui* principles were trendy in Tokyo. Kondo has attributed her passion for tidying to "a desire for recognition from my parents and a complex concerning my mother," in what sounds like a classic case of "middle-child syndrome." She continues, "Because I was poor at developing bonds of trust with people, I had an unusually strong attachment to things." She considers herself an eccentric.

When she was eighteen, Kondo began working at a Shinto shrine. For five years, she sold lucky charms and kept order for the shrine elder. In college, she studied sociology. Her thesis was titled "How to Declutter Your Apartment." According to the *New York Times*, "Kondo recalls that the national library of Japan held a large collection of tidying, decluttering, and organizing books, but it didn't admit anyone under eighteen. Kondo spent her 18th birthday there." She started her home-organizing consulting business the next year, working outside of her full-time job at a staffing agency. Not long after, she quit her day job and began consulting full time. Soon, the wait list for her services reached six months.

Kondo works as a tidying consultant because, in her words, "I want to help others who feel the way I once did, who lack self-confidence and find it hard to open their hearts to others, to see how much support they receive from the space they live in and the things that surround them."

Kondo's popularity in Japan has been compared to that of Beyoncé in the United States, and there was even a Japanese TV movie based on her writings (called *Jinsei ga tokimeku katazuke no mahou*). Kondo's team of handlers has been quoted as anywhere from seven to nine people. Tomohiro Takahashi, the editing director at Sunmark Publishing, which originally published *The Life-Changing Magic of Tidying Up* in Japan, said, "I felt a mysterious energy around her that I had never experienced around other people."

Kondo always wears white, considering it part of her brand. Her "personal power spot" is in a corner of her living room, where she keeps framed photos of her family.

For Your Information

Online

"10 Photos That Illustrate the Healing Power of Organization." EarlyBirdBooks.com

"How Marie Kondo Convinced Me to Stop Shopping." EarlyBirdBooks.com

"Interview with Marie Kondo." GoodReads.com.

"The Japanese art of decluttering and organizing by Marie Kondo." Goop.com

"Kissing Your Socks Goodbye: Home Organization Advice from Marie Kondo." NYTimes.com

"Most Creative People 2015: Marie Kondo." FastCompany.com

"The Origin Story of Marie Kondo's Decluttering Empire." NewYorker.com

"Unexpected Ways Marie Kondo's Book Changed My Life (To The Tune of $10K)." WellandGood.com

"A *Vogue* Editor Learns the Art of Closet-Cleaning From Marie Kondo." Vogue.com

Books

Clutterfree with Kids by Joshua Becker

Do Less: A Minimalist Guide to a Simplified, Organized, and Happy Life by Rachel Jonat

Essentialism: The Disciplined Pursuit of Less by Greg McKeown

The Happiness Project: Or, Why I Spent a Year Trying to Sing in the Morning, Clean My Closets, Fight Right, Read Aristotle, and Generally Have More Fun by Gretchen Rubin

The Joy of Less: A Minimalist Guide—How to Declutter, Organize, and Simplify by Francine Jay

*The Life-Changing Magic of Not Giving a F*ck: How to Stop Spending Time You Don't Have with People You Don't Like Doing Things You Don't Want to Do* by Sarah Knight

Living Well, Spending Less: 12 Secrets of the Good Life by Ruth Soukup

The More of Less: Finding the Life You Want Under Everything You Own by Joshua Becker

New Order: A Decluttering Handbook for Creative Folks (and Everyone Else) by Fay Wolf

Spark Joy: An Illustrated Master Class on the Art of Organizing and Tidying Up by Marie Kondo
Unstuffed: Decluttering Your Home, Mind, and Soul by Ruth Soukup

Bibliography

Brodesser-Akner, Taffy. "Marie Kondo and the Ruthless War on Stuff: The author of 'The Life-Changing Magic of Tidying Up' is embarking on a new venture: training an army of emissaries to declutter the American home." *The New York Times Maazine*, July 6, 2016. http://www.nytimes.com/2016/07/10/magazine/marie-kondo-and-the-ruthless-war-on-stuff.html.

Killingsworth, Silvia. "Shopping at Anthropologie with Marie Kondo." *Culture Desk* (website section), *The New Yorker*, April 27, 2015. http://www.newyorker.com/culture/culture-desk/shopping-at-anthropologie-with-marie-kondo.

KonMari Media. https://konmari.com/consultants/.

Marushima, Motokazu. "What's Sunmark's Formula for Publishing Hits? *The Life-Changing, Pulsing Magic of Cleaning Up:* The Path to Selling Millions. Tomohiro Takahashi, Editing Director, answers this question." Sunmark Publishing's website, 2011. http://www.sunmark.co.jp/eng/newspaper/index.html.

Schoenberg, Nara. "Behind the Zen of decluttering: Why the obsession to get rid of stuff?" *Chicago Tribune,* June 9, 2015. http://www.chicagotribune.com/lifestyles/sc-fam-0616-deciphering-declutter-20150609-story.html.

Silverberg, Nicole. "To Hell and Back Again: A Day with the Marie Kondo Method." *GQ,* April 12, 2016. http://www.gq.com/story/marie-kondo-purge-diary.

Stern, Claire. "Who Is Marie Kondo? 7 Things You Might Not Know About the Japanese Decluttering Guru." *InStyle,* January 23, 2016. http://www.instyle.com/news/marie-kondo-decluttering-queen-trivia.

Young, Molly. "Gurus: Marie Kondo Will Change Your Life . . . Or at least your living space." *The Cut* (website), *New York Magazine,* February 10, 2015. http://nymag.com/thecut/2015/02/marie-kondo-room-purge.html.

MORE SMART SUMMARIES
FROM WORTH BOOKS

SELF-IMPROVEMENT

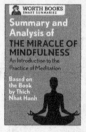

OPEN ROAD

INTEGRATED MEDIA

Find a full list of our authors and
titles at www.openroadmedia.com

FOLLOW US
@OpenRoadMedia